Provence
STYLE OF LIVING

Provence
STYLE OF LIVING

text
JÉRÔME COIGNARD

photographs and captions
MAISONS CÔTÉ SUD

 HACHETTE Illustrated

Introduction

Provence is unique, fascinating, timeless. More than any other region in France, it forms the perfect backdrop for a favourite French pastime, *le bon vivre*. 'The good life' comes easy in Provence; it charms, captivates and inspires, not only by its traditions and culture but also by its rich colours and extraordinary quality of light. Since *Maisons Côté Sud* magazine first appeared in March 1990, we have been privileged to celebrate this beautiful, vital and rich region with its wealth of natural delights, from rolling carpets of lavender to sun-drenched olive groves. We have photographed the country houses, cottages and traditional *mas* of Provence, with their attractively painted walls punctuated by sunlit shutters and set off by box trees in elegant pots. We have discovered their interiors, beautifully restored, reinterpreted and imbued with new life. In this peaceful, serene region you can relax, feel at home and enjoy such delicious local traditions as the ubiquitous *aïoli* (garlic mayonnaise) or a long, lingering Sunday lunch under shady vines. It is a region of diversity and surprises, enchanting in its simple, intimate charm. *Maisons Côté Sud* has published photographs of Provence for over twelve years, revealing its secret gardens, hidden treasures and local delights, the lure of which has reached far beyond its borders. The popularity of Provence has not diminished its appeal – its irresistible charm is both traditional and resolutely contemporary, its style both subtle and audacious. Our magazine's photographers and designers have done their utmost to capture this charm and style in the following pages.

FRANÇOISE LEFÉBURE

Editor in Chief, *Maisons Côté Sud*

Exteriors

Interiors

Exteriors

Mas, bastides and cabanons

'On the way down to the village from my windmill, one passes by a mas, built close to the road, within a courtyard lined with nettle trees. This is a real Provençal dwelling, with its red roof tiles, its broad, brown façade dotted with windows and, perched on the top, the weather vane of the granary […].'

ALPHONSE DAUDET

Previous pages: The Mas des Alpilles is home to American interior designer Ginny Magher. Under her expert eye, the house was renovated, stone by stone, in 18th-century style, by architects Bruno and Alexandre Lafourcade. It has elegant doors and windows, and a huge terrace dappled by the slowly moving shadows of box trees in ceramic pots from St-Jean-de-Fos.
Left: Architect Jean-Paul Bernard's restoration of this 19th-century house combines the traditional style of Vaucluse with subtle touches of Italian inspiration.

'Four houses adorned with orchids up to their roof tiles, emerge from the tall, dense wheat... The wind hums in the plane trees. These are the white bastides.'

JEAN GIONO

From country houses flanked by towers to traditional *mas* and simple cottages, houses in rural Provence are specifically designed to resist the fierce summer heat and turn their backs to the bitterly cold winter winds of the *mistral*. The 18th-century author Nerte Fustier-Dautier said of the Aix region that 'everyone, from members of the aristocracy to the bourgeoisie and working classes, has a house in the country, whether a country house on an estate or a cottage on a small plot of land, where they spend much of their time during the warm summer months. As the days begin to get hotter, the mass exodus from town to country begins.'

Above: The Mas des Songes ('dream farmhouse'), a delightful guest house in Monteux, opens onto the Vaucluse countryside. The harmony of the ochre and lime-rendered exterior exudes a peaceful air of tranquillity.
Left: This old silkworm factory in the department of Var was once an overnight stop for pilgrims bound for Santiago de Compostela. Restored and renovated by architect Claudio Silvestrin, the austere monastic façade blends discreetly with its surroundings.

When we think of a traditional Provençal house, two images immediately spring to mind – the traditional *mas* or farmhouse and the *bastide* or country house. Some might assume that the word *mas* implies a rustic dwelling, a modest farm or smallholding, while *bastide* indicates a more solid and impressive building, even a nobleman's country seat. In fact, nothing could be further from the truth. Some *mas*, dominated by the lofty silhouette of a dovecote, are so large they almost resemble an entire village, huddled around its church, while certain *bastides* are little more than a humble dwelling surrounded by modest outbuildings. Both terms refer to the same thing – an agricultural smallholding, the successor of the Roman villa that incorporated both living accommodation and out-buildings. Each has a diminutive form in French – *mazet* for *mas* and *bastidon* for *bastide* – but

'Dance and Provençal song
and sunburnt mirth!
Oh for a beaker full of
the warm South [...]'

JOHN KEATS

whereas *mas* tends to be used in Arles, western Provence, Bas Languedoc and even Catalonia, *bastide* is more common in eastern Provence. In the department of Vaucluse, the former papal state of the comtat Venaissin (reintegrated into France in 1791), both terms are replaced by *grange* ('barn') or *granjo* in the Provençal dialect. Things become even more complicated with the introduction of the *jas* whose architecture appears to be much the same as that of the *mas* and *bastide*. The term derives from the Latin *jacere* ('to lie down') and originally referred to a farm or sheepfold used for lambing. Some properties retain the name, although the building is more accurately a *mas* or *bastide*.

The restorations carried out by architects Bruno and Alexandre Lafourcade brilliantly capture the authentic style of Provence. Witness the traditional mas (**previous pages**) *whose ochre-painted façade, with its climbing roses and wisteria, is shaded by plane trees, or the old farmhouse (**above, left**) with its traditionally rendered exterior. Rather more modest but just as typical is this delightful cottage (**left**) nestling at the foot of Mont Ventoux.*

Left: This 17th-century Provençal farmhouse in the Drôme has been renovated and restored in traditional style by a firm of eminent Parisian architects, Valode & Pistre, with the invaluable help of Michel Reboulet, a contractor renowned for historic buildings. The rough stone façade gives it all the authentic charm of an old building that has survived the centuries.

Top right: La Guigou is an old mas, nestling in the rural setting of the Val d'Enfer, below the medieval town of Les Baux-de-Provence. It is part of the Domaine de Baumanière, a property that has been doughtily reclaimed from the rocks and scrub of the surrounding landscape. Today the former farmhouse, transformed with passion and dedication by Jean-André and Geneviève Charial, welcomes visitors in search of gastronomic delights and perfect peace and quiet.

One such example is the *Jas de Bouffan* – the former home of the post-Impressionist painter Paul Cézanne – whose grounds are planted with monumental plane trees. The sheep certainly wouldn't recognize this old sheepfold!

For every *mas* and *bastide* there is one or more *cabanons* or 'cots', modest structures isolated amidst crops or vines that have become one of the institutions of Provence. These small, square, one- or two-roomed stone buildings were originally used for storing tools and produce, and sometimes as an overnight shelter, by farmers working on the land. They rarely have a fireplace, but some have a recess or two air vents set in the thickness of the wall. Even so, these functional shelters or basic rural dwellings were often built with great care and their roofs were sometimes decorated with a sort of cornice, known locally as a *génoise*, consisting of three rows of tiles held together with mortar. In the hills, they were built against *restanques*, the terraces that create the region's characteristic landscape of regular terraced fields. These cottages have for a long time been used as weekend retreats. In terms of relative size, the cottage is to the mas what the summerhouse was to the Georgian villa – a place to relax and enjoy the illusion of freedom for a few hours. Old prints testify to the simple joys of this country idyll – anchovies, peppers, tomatoes, broad beans, a few olives and a slice of bread washed down with local wine. Playwright Marcel Pagnol (*Jean de Florette*) immortalized the image of 'Sunday in the country', pervaded by the aroma of *pastis* (aniseed aperitif) and *aïoli* (garlic mayonnaise) as family and friends squeezed onto rustic benches around a table under the vines. Because they were originally too small to serve as

Left: When renovating this beautiful mas *in the Gard department, architect Pierre Cossonnet drew inspiration from traditional buildings and used local materials to blend with the surroundings.* **Following pages:** *This impressive* bastide *has a façade of Vaucluse limestone and a tower with an interior staircase. On a more contemporary note, architect Yves Bayard and designer Jacqueline Morabito have set a white façade against a backdrop of dry stone for this house surrounded by 16th-century* restanques *(terraces).*

proper – or even second – homes, many of these cottages have been extended. From the outside, you can still see the original structure that has been enlarged in the traditional fashion by adding a series of new extensions of varying heights whose roofs are therefore on different levels. Other cottages weren't so fortunate and now stand abandoned, their roofs slowly collapsing, amidst vines and olive trees. Not so the cottages by the sea, where fishermen once mended their nets. These little 'shacks' on the *calanques*, the deep creeks between Marseille and Cassis are deeply coveted and owned by a privileged few. According to a popular saying among local fishermen: 'You may have seen Paris, but if you haven't seen Cassis, you've seen nothing'. The famous architect Le Corbusier paid homage to these modest but idyllic dwellings by building his own cottage at Roquebrune-Cap-Martin in the early 1950s.

Tiled roofs

Provençal roofs are covered with the characteristic half-round tiles known as *romaines* – one of the legacies of the Roman occupation. Their rich terracotta colour is part of the warm, earthy palette that makes the region's houses blend so perfectly with the landscape. Each elevation has its own roof, which is never on the same level as the one next to it. Generally speaking, roofs are low pitched – between 20° and 30° – since protection against rain is not a priority. Furthermore, as houses were built chiefly by stonemasons, the roof timbers are often a very basic framework – just enough to hold the heavy, rather slippery tiles in place. The eaves are sometimes supported by a *génoise*, a sort of cornice consisting of three rows of tiles held together with mortar. In the past, given the simplicity of the façades of even the most luxurious houses, it was the quality of the tiles that reflected the social status of the owner. But these tiles are functional as well as decorative since, by extending the overhang of the eaves, they keep rainwater away from the walls. Chimneys come in all shapes and finishes but are generally built on the thick, north-facing wall carrying the gutter at the back of the house. In Haute-Provence chimney flues are often covered with a tiled hood or cowl as a safeguard against bad weather. They also tend to be placed against an internal partition wall. This not only means they can heat several rooms at the same time, but also prevents the bitterly cold winter wind, the famous *mistral*, from suddenly cooling the flue and thereby affecting the draw.

In Provence, roofs are a key element in the region's rich palette of colours and the quality of its reflected light. Here are some superb examples of roofs covered with weathered terracotta tiles.
Right: The roof of this beautifully renovated old farmhouse in the Luberon mountains is covered with the characteristic half-round tiles of Provence.

From burnt umber to yellow ochre, the pigments of the Luberon mountains colour the walls of houses throughout Provence with their warm earthy tones, as shown in this façade restored by B. & A. Lafourcade (**left**) and the red-ochre walls of a Mediterranean country house designed by Maurice Savinel and Roland Le Bévillon (**opposite, right**). But stone has lost none of its appeal and attests to the authenticity of an 18th-century farmhouse (**below**).

Stone and rendering

The façades of Provençal houses – even those with richly decorated interiors – are usually very soberly and simply designed, a simplicity that was actively encouraged by the French nobility, such as Victor de Riqueti, Marquis de Mirabeau, father of the famous French statesman and orator, who, in the 18th century, counselled his brother: 'Just as you don't follow fashion for your hairstyle, do not follow it for your château. Build it to suit yourself, that's all.' With the exception of the Camargue, Provence is a region of stone whose colour varies depending on where it is quarried, the grey stone from La Roche d'Espeil being prized for its regular grain, while the warm amber-coloured stone quarried at Rognes was used in the distinctive façades and monuments of Aix-en-Provence. Stone from Les Baux is much whiter in colour, Ménerbes stone is rich in fossils deposited by the sea millions of years ago, and the stone from Cassis is incredibly hard. Often, there was no need to source building materials from the region's major quarries since farmers could build their houses from the 'quarry' on their own land: freestone blocks for the door and window frames and small, irregular stones held together with mortar for the walls. The lime rendering used to cover the walls takes on the colour of the earth or sand mixed with it – mainly white in Mediterranean regions, while the façades of inland Provence reflect a rich and varied palette of colours ranging from yellow ochre to raw sienna and burnt umber. Its composition varies depending on the number of crushed tiles used and the amount of ochre – the fine powder used by the Romans and rediscovered in the 18th century – added to the mortar. The colour of ochre, formed from marine sediments from which the sand is removed, is due to the presence of iron oxide. It is dried in the sun for a month, but only acquires its red colour after being fired in a kiln at over 500°C (932 °F).

Doors, windows and shutters

'*I adore your letters from Avignon, my darling: I read and re-read them […] thus enjoying your fine sunshine, the charming banks of your handsome Rhône, the sweetness of your air […].*'

MADAME DE SÉVIGNÉ

A leafy vine hung with ripening grapes filters the sun's rays, rampart-like walls resist the onslaught of the summer heat and windows are shaded by solid wood shutters. In the strange lethargy that envelops the region and its inhabitants during the hottest hours of the day, the country houses of Provence jealously preserve the cool freshness of their interiors. Windows and doors always open to the south since the north side of the house must be impervious to the region's bitterly cold winter winds, the *mistral* and *montagnière*. This is a rule that is wise to observe since, according to Lanéry d'Arc, the author of a book on Provençal houses published in the late 19th century, 'in Provence, windows never close properly'.

Solid wood shutters are often the only decorative element on Provençal façades. On the more elaborate shutters, the solid panel on the lower half has been replaced by wooden slats that can be opened and closed by means of an iron bar or a sliding batten. These 'peepholes' allow you to look out without being seen and also let in air and light while providing protection against the summer heat. There are also classic louvered shutters with fixed slats and the solid wood shutters of traditional farmhouses.

The colour of the external woodwork – shutters, doors and windows – provides a contrast to the soft, warm tones of the stone or rendered façade. Greens are popular, from the beautiful dark 'cypress' green to lighter shades somewhere between evergreen oak and olive trees.

Provence is also often associated with the colour blue because of its rolling fields of lavender. But this could equally well be due to the colour of its shutters, which range from the strong *bleu charrette* to lavender blue, and from the glorious azure of Cézanne's skies to pastel blue. Blue also has the advantage of keeping away flies. Finally, red is found in a variety of shades and is the third most popular colour used for painting external woodwork. It is also the oldest, since it dates from the Middle Ages, although it is now less widely used than blue and green.

*Whether they are in 18th-century classical style (**previous pages**) or the solid stone of a former village school in the Vaucluse (**left**), Provençal doors have a charm all their own. 'Shutters are the eyelids of summer' wrote the 20th-century French author Yvan Audouard. Solid wood shutters (**above, left**) or shutters with movable slats (**above, right**) reflect the style of the house.*

Another, much more recent tradition that has become popular throughout the region is the use of the *rideau marseillais*, a sort of door curtain (*below*) made of turned boxwood beads threaded onto long lengths of wire. Some have geometric patterns created by the alternate use of stained and plain varnished beads. These curtains allow the air to circulate while keeping sunlight and winged insects at bay. Sometimes windows and doors were – and in some cases still are – fitted with an inner mesh framework or mosquito door.

In the past, doors and interior woodwork were painted with oil-based paints that often matched the colour of the shutters. Natural wood, whether stained, waxed or varnished, is simply unheard of in traditional Provençal houses. Only wooden furniture is allowed to retain its natural appearance but even that has to be given an exceptional patina by the application of successive layers of a good beeswax polish.

*Opposite page: La Bastide, a guest house at the foot of the Alpilles mountains, has pastel-coloured walls. **Left:** At the first sign of hot weather, boxwood door curtains waft gently in the breeze. Above: Louvered door shutters filter heat and sunlight. **Following pages:** Elegant serenity viewed through the French windows of a house in Uzès (**left**), and (**right**) in the Grasse region, an arched window frames a picturesque terrace bathed in beautifully mottled light.*

Below left: An overgrown wrought-iron gateway marks the entrance to this mas in the Alpilles mountains.
Right: Wrought-iron railings in the Musée Souleiado in Tarascon.
Below right: This high wrought-iron gate, once one of the crowning glories of a chateau in the Aix region, is a striking contrast to the red-ochre façade.
Opposite: In the Bastide de Moustiers, a reclaimed wrought-iron grille with a 'sun' design is in keeping with the monochrome of the yellow-ochre floor tiles and 19th-century dresser.

The art of
wrought ironwork

In the past, wrought-iron craftsmen were highly respected in Provence. They were skilled artisans who knew how to get the best from their material and Provençal church spires were original works of art that had the added advantage of offering low wind resistance in a region swept by the *mistral*. In the 17th century, their art was turned to secular account as the mansions of Aix-en-Provence, Carpentras and Toulon were decorated with lacy wrought ironwork by master craftsmen like Giraud, Duval and Poussin. The craft was at its height during the reign of Louis XV (1715–74), which produced such masterpieces as the staircases and balconies by Alexis Benoît in the Hôtel Forbin Sainte-Croix (now the *préfecture*) in Avignon. However, the region's wealthy citizens also commissioned wrought ironwork for their country houses and there were few gardens or country estates that did not have an impressive wrought-iron gateway in pure 17th-century style. Soft steel was used to decorate their work with scrolls that concealed the inevitable rivets and soldering, and thus wrought-iron craftsmen moved away from their original and more utilitarian craft – the manufacture of hinges.

Nowadays their creations combine the two characteristics of wrought ironwork – strength and elegance. On some houses, the traditional Provençal shutters have been replaced by Spanish-style wrought-iron grilles whose decorative elegance quite belies their protective role. Similarly, gardens are graced by elegant wrought-iron pergolas – decorative elements that can withstand the onslaughts of wisteria and the vagaries of the seasons, designed by artisans who are certainly masters of their craft.

Mediterranean gardens

'Oh , light! Now I know
what the Provençal
garden is: it's the garden
which needs nothing to
surpass all others except
to grow in Provence.'

COLETTE

From Mont Ventoux to the Mediterranean coast, the hillsides of Provence form a sculpted landscape of regular terraced fields. Hundreds of years ago, these *restanques* or terraces were carved out of the hillside by a backbreaking process of digging and banking, a massive undertaking that made it possible to plough and cultivate steep slopes that were previously impossible to farm. They were built by skilled labourers known as *emparadaires* or *muraillaires* (wallers). Nowadays these terraces lend structure to the countless gardens that occupy the strips of land or *bancaux* where wheat, vines and flowers, especially around the perfume town of Grasse, were once – and in some places still are – grown.

For centuries, this rocky landscape has supported natural vegetation that can withstand the intense summer heat and winter downpours.

Provençal gardens are characterized by the presence of two trees with very distinctive personalities – the olive, which can live for several hundred years, and the cypress. A legend that may have originated in the writings of the Roman historian Justin – Marcus Junianus Justinus (*fl.* 3rd century AD) – attributes the introduction of the olive tree to the ancient Greeks. According to classical mythology, it was a gift from the goddess Athena. However, research has revealed that the wild olive was growing in Provence long before the arrival of the first Greek settlers and that it was probably grafted and cultivated by the Phoenicians.

Left: The green architecture of restanques punctuated by cypresses near Grasse, and (above) a 19th-century 'swan' bench, an ideal place to spend a few quiet moments with a book.
Following pages: Beyond an old wrought-iron gate, pathways bordered by fragrant lavender and clipped yew hedges lead to the old-style kitchen garden of the Château Val-Joanis in the Luberon mountains.

As well as being an integral part of the Provençal landscape, the ubiquitous olive tree is also increasingly widely used in private gardens for its ornamental qualities and characteristic silver-grey evergreen foliage. Its low-growing, open habit and light, airy foliage provide a striking contrast to the erect, slender outline and dense, dark-green foliage of the cypress. This ardent sun-worshipper, with its distinctive silhouette, recalls Tuscany whose famous son, the lyric poet and scholar Petrarch, had a long and memorable stay in Provence. Closely planted – sometimes double or treble – cypress hedges create an impenetrable barrier against the strong winds of the *mistral*. Of all Provençal hedges – blackthorn, wild rose and hawthorn, wild pomegranate and berberis – the cypress hedge is the most monumental and most impressive. However, the cypress is not the only conifer to thrive in Mediterranean gardens

and other species include the Aleppo and maritime pines whose curved silhouette is widely found in coastal regions.

Traditionally, the estates of the nobility were planted with a pinetum, a deliciously cool and shady place to walk during the hottest hours of the day when the symmetrical patchwork of French-style flowerbeds was exposed to the blazing sun. Another ideal place for a quiet to stroll was the *tèse*, a series of tree-covered walks and the classic counterpart of the pinetum. However, the origins of the *tèse* are less romantic – it was originally designed to trap small birds, destined for the spit, by means of a huge net thrown across the walk. Today the

Opposite: The Souviou estate, on the western slopes of the Var department, is renowned for the quality of its wines. In a garden shaded by plane trees, where the air is pervaded by heady aromas, the 16th-century country house has retained all its old-fashioned charm.
Above: In this orangery in the Alpilles mountains, avocado, lemon and orange trees are grown in containers. The exterior is decorated with Chinese motifs and set off by a palm tree and geraniums planted in beautiful Anduze vases.

tèse has virtually disappeared and only a few can still be seen, for example in the 18th-century Albertas gardens, in Bouc-Bel-Air, near Aix-en-Provence, and at the Château de la Gaude, near Grasse.

Planting a *tèse* was not something to be undertaken lightly. Records show that, in 1765, Honoré Roux planted a new *tèse* on his country estate near Antignane, consisting of 113 rows of six different trees – laurustinus, terebinth, fig, hawthorn, ash and tamarind – planted alternately. These elaborate structures were punctuated by garden 'rooms' furnished with stone benches and statues.

The Provençal *garrigue* or scrubland is a far cry from the aristocratic elegance of this type of planting. Its stony soil supports a wide variety of predominately evergreen shrubs and bushes which, from time immemorial, have struggled to survive the combined onslaught of *mistral* and sun.

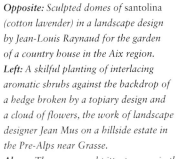

Opposite: Sculpted domes of santolina *(cotton lavender) in a landscape design by Jean-Louis Raynaud for the garden of a country house in the Aix region.*
Left: A skilful planting of interlacing aromatic shrubs against the backdrop of a hedge broken by a topiary design and a cloud of flowers, the work of landscape designer Jean Mus on a hillside estate in the Pre-Alps near Grasse.
Above: The agaves and pittosporums in this garden at Gassin near St Tropez were planted by landscape designer and nurseryman Thierry Derbez.

As a result, they grow low and squat so as to stay firmly rooted in the soil. Holm-oak, cork oak, cade, juniper, pistachio, terebinth, mastic and laurustinus grow naturally in the region and form the basic framework of many Provençal gardens. Shaggy shrubs such as thyme, rosemary, lavender and cistus (rock rose) are well suited to stony ground and rock gardens, their small leaves and tiny flowers attesting to the aridity of the soil in which they grow. In a climate where English-style lawns struggle to survive, the irregular shapes and heights of their rounded clumps provide the flesh and substance of the garden. Modern gardeners tend to create contrast by alternating them with softer foliage and fleshy plants.

On a hillside near Grasse, protected from the mistral *and irrigated with mountain water, the garden of this 17th-century country house with rose-coloured walls was restored by landscape designer Jean Mus. The steps are planted with* Polygonum capitatum *(pink knotweed) and edged with* Convolvulus cneorum *(bush morning glory), vittadinia and clumps of box. Under olive trees and Banks roses, helichrysums mingle with* Agathaea coelestis *(blue marguerite) and pittosporums.*

Greenhouse effects …
Left: This orangery, with its reclaimed, arched French window, protects tender shrubs and trees planted in Anduze vases.
Above: This elegant 1880s greenhouse was restored by Aix architect Jean-Paul Bernard.
Right: In front of this neo-classical orangery, date palms, agaves and yuccas bask in the sun under the watchful eye of a grotesque by Spigo Toscano.

In the interests of contrast, Jean Mus has
helped to extricate the long-stemmed euphorbia
with its clusters of greenish-yellow flowers from
the damning category of weeds, while tropical
plants have flourished on the Côte d'Azur for
over a century. The exuberant foliage of royal
palms, banana trees and eucalyptus, and the
sharp-toothed leaves of Mexican agaves have
become the symbol of the sun-drenched coast of
Provence.

The scent of lavender and rose

Provençal gardens are first and foremost a symphony of scents and perfumes. Enjoy their fragrance by closing your eyes and breathing in the rich, spicy aromas, then let yourself be soothed by their pure lines and the depth and harmony of their colours. What could be more inviting than to relax in the shade of solid stone walls on a hot summer's afternoon when only the cicadas brave the heat and the air vibrates to the sound of their endless chirring? In the warmth of the sun, plants and flowers release their fragrances – the heady perfume of jasmine mingles with the aromatic fragrance of plants from the *garrigue* and the invigorating scent of lavender, while pines give off a smooth, resinous aroma, figs release their rich, honey-sweet perfume and box adds a woody note. Not forgetting the fragrance of the famous, sensuous *Rosa centifolia*, once the pride of the hillsides around the town of Grasse, mecca of perfume-makers from around the world. Grasse, with its narrow, winding streets, is perched high on a rocky outcrop above fertile plains that were once covered with a thick carpet of flowers – roses, violets, daffodils, mignonettes and tuberoses. Capturing their scent involved lengthy and complex techniques since some, like jasmine and hyacinth, could not withstand the harsh heat of the stills. In his book *Perfume*, Patrick Süskind evokes all the poetry of the art of perfume making .

The symbols of
Provence – olive trees,
rolling fields of
lavender and air
heavy with the scent
of roses. 'Sénateur
Lafolette', a beautiful
hybrid tea rose and
vigorous climber,
twines around the
trunk of an old pear
tree (**right**).

In Grasse, they know how to capture the essence of flowers. The distillery floor of the Fragonard perfumery is strewn with cinnamon roses, which once arrived by the ton (*above and opposite page, bottom*). Lavender is woven into hearts and 'bobbins' to slip into linen chests (*opposite page, top*) or lends its fragrance to pot-pourri, lavender bags, terracotta medallions and soaps.

The technique of *enfleurage* involves exposing odourless fats and oils to the fragrance of fresh flowers by spreading flowers on slabs of solidified fats or wrapping them carefully in cotton fabric steeped in odourless oils. They are later removed and replaced by a fresh batch of flowers, a process that is repeated until the fats or oils are saturated with their perfume.

Lavender or, more accurately, hybrid lavender, which adds a touch of purplish blue to the stark Provence described by novelist Jean Giono, does not require such careful handling. It is picked without ceremony, using modern machinery, at the height of the summer flowering season. After a fairly perfunctory drying in the sun, bunches of lavender – flowers, stalks and all – are forked into huge metal containers, which are hermetically sealed and sent to the distillery. Here steam injected into the containers becomes saturated with essential oils from the lavender. These are separated out when the steam is cooled in a condensing coil. In the 17th century, the Marquise de Sévigné – whose famous letters to her daughter recounted all the news and gossip of fashionable society – introduced the use of lavender to the royal court. She favoured Hungary water, a type of cologne made from lavender, rosemary and marjoram. 'It is divine,' she wrote. 'I keep it in my pocket and its perfume intoxicates me daily.' She likened it to an addiction to tobacco in the sense that, once you have used it, you simply cannot do without it. Mme de Sévigné also recommended the daily use of unguents based on lavender oils and bitter almonds as a flea and lice repellent. But it was not until the 18th century that the use of lavender became widespread and the consumption of essence of lavender reached an all-time high. The only way to prevent prices spiralling out of control was to increase production significantly and this led to the use of foreign labour. However, the first great lavender plantations, known as *lavanderaies*, did not appear until the 1920s, giving a new lease of life to high-plateau areas that had hitherto been regarded as uncultivable.

Ponds, pools and fountains

*' In the middle of the
square an old fountain
spread its stomach. [...]
Four marble-cheeked
cherubs with distended
mouths blew pipes – but
the water didn't flow.
Nevertheless, the fountain
was full of clear water;
its riches spilling over
onto the paving stones.'*

JEAN GIONO

What could be more attractive and relaxing than water splashing gently into a fountain or flowing into a stone-edged pond or pool? But water is also a source of life that once gave rise to bitter rivalries and even crimes in this region – conflicts vividly evoked by Marcel Pagnol in *Jean de Florette*, filmed by Claude Berri in 1986. No wonder water diviners were often the subject of rumours and wild fantasies, sometimes even regarded as magicians. In the past, houses were built in rural Provence only if close to a water supply – a spring or underground stream that could be tapped by digging a well. Today there is no shortage of water in the gardens of the region's country houses, where it is often used to create spectacular effects.

Previous pages: Maurice Savinel and Roland Le Bévillon drew inspiration for this pool from old-fashioned irrigation tanks. Edged with 18th-century paving slabs from Chabaus, in Apt, the stone-coloured waterproof rendered lining creates natural reflections.
Above: A pool surrounded by old stone and guarded by mythological beasts in a timeless garden near the town of Grasse.
Opposite: Landscape designer Dominique Lafourcade has made a stunning feature of an old water tank by encasing it in skilfully 'aged' stone from Les Baux-de-Provence.

In the 18th century, hydraulic engineers and master plumbers designed complex systems of underground galleries, pipes, conduits and tanks that collected water from springs and streams and channelled it into pools and fountains on Provençal country estates. A fine example of these masterpieces of hydraulic engineering is the pool with seventeen fountains in the Albertas gardens, in the village of Bouc-Bel-Air near Aix-en-Provence. Created during the reign of Louis XV (1715–74), its sculpted Tritons still blow fine jets of water from their conch-shell trumpets, to the delight and amazement of modern visitors. But even the most modest farmhouses can harness water from one or two springs and create a magical effect with the smallest and simplest of fountains – a stone hydrant, a rectangular tank or a tap decorated with a graceful swan's neck. In an arid landscape where water is at a premium, the gentle murmur of these simple fountains is worth all the most elaborate hydraulic systems and spectacular effects in the world.

In the past, ornamental pools were the prerogative of stately homes and the modest water supply of a traditional farmhouse would certainly not have been enough to sustain such an elaborate feature. Although

Above: In the hills near Nice, olive trees encircle a travertine-edged pool filled to overflowing.
Left: This swimming pool designed by Jacqueline Morabito is set into a restanque *(terrace)*. The concrete interior and edges have a silicate-marble coating tinged with a blend of grey and sand so that the water takes on the colour of the surrounding olive trees.
Opposite: This swimming pool in the Apt region is designed to create a perfect blend of stone and vegetation by the use of Ménerbes stone and neatly clipped shrubs.

modern Provençal gardens make increasing use of water for decorative and ornamental effect, this fashion is inspired less by the impressive elegance of elaborate pools and fountains than by the growing trend for comfort and *al fresco* living. Nowadays most holiday homes and restored farmhouses in the region have – or dream of having – a swimming pool. The very mention of the word conjures up images of a landscape marred by a glaringly white stone surround and outrageous paintwork that gives the water an unnatural tropical-blue colour – the symbols of Californian overkill in the South of France. However if designed to blend with their natural surroundings and make use of local materials, pools can provide a harmonious complement to the Provençal garden while adding the luxury only dreamed of by previous generations – a plentiful supply of water.

A simple, rectangular pool edged with local stone – with an interior painted in the muted tones of old fountains, rather than the bright tropical blue that not even deep water can soften – will blend harmoniously with its surroundings and add to rather than detract from the garden landscape.

*The delightful murmur of water in the gardens of the Galerie Lestranger (**left**) and the Château Val-Joanis (**right**).*

Pools are best located on the main south-facing side of the house so that they are protected against the adverse effects of the *mistral*. They can be surrounded by traditional low walls or a series of strategically planted shrubs. Alternatively, a *restanque*, one of the region's long, narrow terraces, makes an ideal site for a pool. Gardens with a view of the sea can create optical illusions, by means of an overflow system that gives the impression of a natural link between pool and sea. What better introduction to a Provençal garden than to dive into an exquisitely refreshing pool in the height of summer and contemplate the intense blue of a sky worthy of Cézanne?

An Italian-style fountain near Grasse *(above, left)* and a gently murmuring stone fountain in the Luberon mountains *(above)*. **Opposite:** *An old irrigation tank skilfully transformed into a reservoir-fountain by Maurice Savinel and Roland Le Bévillon.* **Following pages:** *The dry-stone boundary wall and huge Cretan urns from Vive le Jardin, in Aix-en-Provence, are reflected in the waters of this pool overlooking the famous Mont Sainte-Victoire, painted by Cézanne.*

Above: *Two magnificent 18th- and 19th-century terracotta storage jars from Biot stand on either side of the entrance of the Mas dou Pastre, a former sheepfold now converted into a hotel, in the hilltop village of Eygalières.*

Left: *Rows of generously curved pots in the Poterie Ravel, in Aubagne, established in 1837.*

Right: *A special trolley is used to bring Anduze vases inside for the winter. The vases are still manufactured according to a traditional 16th-century method.*

Top, opposite: *An Anduze vase signed by the famous potter Jean Gautier in 1816.*

Right, opposite: *Glazed gadrooned vases from the Poterie de la Madeleine, in Anduze.*

Garden pots and urns

Terracotta jars discovered near the village of Salernes-en-Provence are thought to be around 7,000 years old and the oldest in Western Europe. These huge jars were not only used for storing liquids – water, wine and oil – but also dry goods. They were used to store grain and flour on farms or as containers for these precious commodities on board ship and, as such, are the perfect symbol of the agricultural and commercial side of Provence. Although these jars have been replaced by the storage facilities of modern industry they are now highly prized for their decorative qualities, a new role that has given them a new lease of life. Nowadays they stand proudly in traditional Mediterranean-style gardens where their generous curves are a symbol of abundance and hopefully a good omen for the plants growing there. From the Middle Ages, the region around the town of Biot – rich in clay, sand, manganese, wood and flint – has been one of the centres of monumental pottery. As in potteries throughout France, the jars and amphorae made in Biot are characterized by their plain terracotta exteriors and glazed interiors. Their shape is ideally suited to trailing plants but since they were originally designed for storing olive oil and wine, there are no holes in the bottom.

While the jars made in Biot had a simple, practical function, Anduze vases were designed specifically as garden ornaments. They may have been derived from elegant Roman urns decorated with plant motifs, and the urn shape is very characteristic. These vases are varnished inside and out in ochre or green and decorated with floral garlands and medallions bearing the maker's mark.

Vines and the art of shade

'The great grave house, [of which] the back, invisible to the passer-by, and gilded by the sun, was covered in wisteria and begonia entwined together, lying heavily on the worn iron trellis, sagging in the middle like a hammock, that sheltered the little paved terrace and the windowsill of the sitting room.'

COLETTE

Provençal terraces are an extension of the south-facing façade of the house. Throughout the summer, they are both literally and figuratively the focal point of domestic life, being sheltered from the *mistral* by the body of the house and protected from the relentless summer sun by a vine arbour or trellis. This is usually supported by a wrought-iron framework and sometimes by stone or masonry supports, while the thick foliage of an old wisteria or a gnarled vine creates a haven of leafy freshness and shades the house from the summer heat. Occasionally, bignonia, a tropical climber, adds its orange trumpets to the purple of muscat grapes.

'We chase dreams and embrace shadows.'
ANATOLE FRANCE

Solid stone benches set against the façade, a heavy stone table and a few chairs complete the setting for a delightful garden room. The kitchen door is never far away and meals are served and eaten *al fresco*. Near the coast, the air may well be heavy with the scent of orange, mandarin and lemon trees planted in pots. Huge terracotta jars, originally used for storing food, and garden pots made from local clay provide a striking contrast to the shiny green glaze of Anduze vases from Languedoc. Pelargoniums, whose leaves release their scent at the slightest touch, give off fragrances of mint or citrus and, like lavender, keep unwanted insects at bay.

Provençal terraces are often shaded by trees, sometimes a lime or an old mulberry (whose leaves were once used to feed silk worms) but generally by plane trees as their shade is said to be cooler, which is why, although not introduced into Provence until the 1830s, plane trees are now widespread throughout the region.

Left: At the Bastide de Moustiers, the kitchen garden of chef Alain Ducasse provides a freshly picked lunch of salad, herbs and early spring vegetables.
Above, left: On a terrace near Grasse, chestnut-wood chairs invite relaxation in the softly dappled shade of a climbing vine.

With their mottled, ochre and grey trunks, beautifully structured branches and abundant foliage, plane trees adorn many a square and boulevard in Provençal towns, shade petanque malls and line the driveways of large country houses. Planted on a terrace at the front of a house, they are pruned and trained into shapes that are not only spectacular but also effective in providing shade from the sun – the vertical branches are removed and the horizontal branches joined together using canes tied with willow. After a few years they create a wonderful shady arbour known locally as an *ombrière*. Fig trees, with their large, dark-green, hand-shaped leaves are also popular but are usually relegated to a far corner of the garden as their shade is – quite wrongly – considered to be unhealthy. If you haven't experienced the pleasure of stretching out your hand to pick a ripe, juicy fig as you recline on a sun lounger, you haven't lived!

Above: *An al fresco lunch in the shade of mulberry trees, on the terrace of an 18th-century country house in Haut-Var, restored by designer Susie Manby, or under a vine arbour pervaded by the heady scent of lavender (**left**).*
Opposite: *Dining under the vines at the home of the renowned Provençal chef Reine Sammut is a delicious experience.*
Following pages: *The simplicity of a vine arbour in the Vaucluse, with reproduction chairs by Hervé Baume (**left**), and a delightful setting for dinner at the Bastide de Marie, in Ménerbes (**right**).*

The terrace is a Provençal institution, which in stately homes assumes the vast proportions of an impressive platform with a commanding view of the grounds. These terraces are usually surrounded by a stone balustrade or wrought-iron railings and decorated with sculpted vases and statues. In the 17th and 18th centuries, they overlooked intricate and ornate box-tree topiaries, examples of which can still be seen at the Château de la Gaude, near Aix-en-Provence, and the Château de Beauregard, near Mons. The full shapes and dense foliage of the box trees, clipped into knots and orbs, offset the profusion of stone ornaments – inspired by Italian villas and the Château de Versailles – scattered throughout the grounds. Once again, stone provides structure and order, but even the most sophisticated gardens never lose sight of the elegant simplicity that is the inspiration and leitmotif of Provençal style.

Wattle screens

Made from Provençal canes cut lengthways and dried in the sun, these screens are an inexpensive and attractive way of creating shade. Originally used by the ancient Egyptians, they are still widely found in Mediterranean regions where they became popular as a means of providing softly dappled shade for all kinds of dwellings, from humble cottages to elegant country houses. Their tightly woven texture makes them light and strong, and they can be rolled and unrolled according to the season and position of the sun. Apart from providing welcoming shade, they can also be used as a windbreak against the mistral or as a screen from prying eyes, while some even have a Virginia creeper or clematis scrambling over them.

Left: *An 18th-century-style wrought-iron gateway framed by honeysuckle and Virginia creeper at Château Val-Joanis, near Pertuis.*
Above: *Light and shade on an 18th-century mosaic stone paving.*
Below: *A handsome old wheelbarrow filled with rose petals at the Musée Fragonard in Grasse.*
Opposite: *Cement tiles with a characteristic fillet and cabochon design, from Marina de Baleine.*

Mosaic stone paving

Since Roman times, access to hillside farms has been by way of simple paths with broad, gently sloping steps. These pathways could be used on foot, on horseback or on a donkey and saved people and animals from getting bogged down in ground made soft and muddy by the constant flow of rainwater. They were surfaced with stones and cobbles held in place by other, heavier stones and covered with earth. As the earth was gradually compacted, the cobbles began to reappear, creating an irregular surface that provided extra purchase and reduced the risk of slipping. This very practical surface became known as mosaic stone paving or *caladon* in the Provençal dialect. Its toughness and the ease with which it is laid has made it one of the basic elements in the region's architectural repertoire, all the more so since Provence has a plentiful supply of stones and cobbles. Washed down by streams and tumbled by rivers, these stones also abound on plateaux such as the Plateau de Valensole, whose southern edge runs along the valley of the Verdon River, and plains like the Grande Crau, the southern part of the vast plain of the Crau, once the delta of the Durance. These smooth and attractive stones are used on a massive scale and their aesthetic quality is much appreciated. They are employed to make terraces, in wall motifs, as paving, for example in towns like Avignon, and even for interior flooring, where they create a picturesque effect. The *caladon* is extremely versatile in terms of form and colour – for example, creating wave patterns and spirals – and makes floors a decorative element in their own right, a fashion that appears to have been imported from Italy and the Ligurian province of Genoa in particular.

Interiors

Entrances and stairways

' […] these houses reveal
harmonious stairways
and rooms where the old
Provençal way of life under
its kings is almost intact.
And all that silence,
those proportions, those
handsome, hidden rooms,
suited to a life of study,
even idleness, should one
choose it, exude order, the
wisdom of lives in balance.'

ANDRÉ SUARÈS

Previous pages: This stairway is a fine example of the art of masonry, with the handrail an integral part of the banister.
Below: The hallway of this 18th-century mill in the Alpilles mountains opens onto the kitchen.
Left: In the Vaucluse, the restrained elegance of a staircase whose sweeping lines are highlighted by a simple wooden handrail set on wrought-iron banister rails.
Opposite: A staircase whose steps have been worn down with use emphasizes the architectural asymmetry of this farmhouse in the Gard.

The shape and size of Provençal farmhouses varies considerably depending on the wealth of their successive owners, the region and the type of terrain on which they were built. They are often modest, rectangular buildings that have been gradually extended over the years by the addition of a series of simple lean-tos – a sheepfold, bread oven, pigsty, shed, henhouse. These successive extensions often form an L or U shape, or even an enclosed farmyard, at least on the plains where building is not constrained by the slope of the land. Sometimes interior doors open directly into these outbuildings whose conversion into living space has left picturesque traces of the original layout – different levels that require steps between one room and the next, or thick exterior walls that are now incorporated into the building. Some outbuildings, such as the sheepfold or pigsty, had to be reached from outside, an apparent disadvantage that can in fact add an element of unusual charm and surprise to a restored farmhouse. The layout of Provençal houses suggests that most

had interior staircases. These were usually single-flight, stone stairways but they could also be curved or have two or three flights, turning at a corner angle of the house. In northern Provence, however, especially in the Alpes-de-Haute-Provence, staircases were often on the exterior and led to a porch or *pountin* that was sometimes covered and gave access to the house.

The Provençal tradition of sober interior walls is immediately obvious as you enter the house. In the past, walls were quite simply whitewashed once a year. While this was being done – strangely enough, by the womenfolk – all furniture and fittings were removed from the room. The *Maison rustique ou recueil de tout ce qui peut servir au ménage de la campagne* – a collection of handy hints for rural households published in 1720 – recommended adding crushed river pebbles, 'a few well-beaten

Opposite: The sobriety of this white-painted staircase is set off by coloured niches and cornices.
Above: A simple stone staircase in a 17th-century château, leading to a series of rooms whose walls are painted with 'eggshell' distemper.
Left: The clean, curved lines of this flight of stairs, in an old mill near Grasse, provide a chromatic counterpoint to the patina of a waxed oil jar.

egg whites' and even goat's fat to the sieved quicklime. Coloured pigments – yellow-ochre, green or light blue – were often added to the distemper and, so that scuffmarks were less noticeable, the base of the wall was painted a darker colour. Nowadays lime-based distempers are back in fashion. They are popular for their matt finish, their simple, basic ingredients and slightly irregular texture. Mixed with pigments, they can produce effects that evoke the transparency of watercolours. The tedious preparation process, made dangerous by the use of quicklime, has been considerably simplified and improved by modern manufacturers.

Opposite: The treads of this flight of stairs in a house in the Grasse region are edged with old half-inch planks.
Above: The magnificently restored entrance hall of the Château de Moissac, in Haut-Var, has retained the floor of local flagstone, and the 17th-century staircase its plasterwork.
Above, left: A staircase painted in soft monochrome tones leads to a bedroom in the Bastide de Marie.

Terracotta
floor tiles...

Terracotta floor tiles, known locally as *malouns*, are the most popular form of flooring in Provençal houses. They are cool, hardwearing and easy to wash down. Their warm colour varies according to the type of clay used, usually that of the region where they are made. The village of Salernes-en-Provence is still a major centre for the manufacture of terracotta tiles even though only fifteen of its eighty or so tileries have survived. Its former prosperity was due to a plentiful supply of the three raw materials vital to the industry – clay, water and wood. In the past, the tiles were made entirely by hand and involved a number of skilled craftsmen and women. The *pastonneur* (kneader) removed impurities and kneaded the lumps of clay or *pâtons*, the *malonneur* removed any air bubbles, flattened the clay and used a wooden frame to cut the tiles or *malouns*, while the *rabateuse* (smoother) polished the tiles and the *coupeuse* (cutter) cut them to the required shape and size. Finally, the *enfourneur* (kiln-man) fired the tiles in the kiln, a process that could take over a week.

Square tiles were once the most widely used but were superseded by the hexagonal tiles known as *tomettes*, whose shape continues to be the best known and most typical of the region. Triangular and octagonal tiles, which have existed for as long as the *tomettes*, were also once

Above and opposite: In the Salernes workshop of craftsman Maurice Emphoux, three generations of *tomettes*, showing the different shades of their red slip, are stacked outside the kiln.
Below: Tile flooring being laid at the Chaource home of Jean Courtine, designer and maker of hand-made terracotta tiles. Some of the tiles are inlaid with geometric and plant motifs.
Bottom right: Old *tomettes* cover the floors of this former private mansion, now the antique shop of Frédéric Dervieux, in Arles.

... and cement tiles

extremely popular. However, like square tiles, they gradually sank into oblivion, only recently being rehabilitated by decorators intent on reviving regional traditions.

Cement tiles suffered a similar fate since they tended to be associated with the 'poor' style of post-war reconstruction years and remained very much in the background for the next twenty years or so. However, this type of flooring is just as attractive and representative of Provençal tradition as the *tomettes*. Cement tiles were first manufactured in the mid-19th century in the great cement works of the Ardèche region and were rapidly adopted by architects working in and around Avignon. The undeniable resilience and toughness of cement, combined with its aesthetic qualities, meant that the popularity of this material was more than a passing trend – witness the fact that there are still craftsmen taking commissions for hand-made cement tiles today. It is also possible to add all kinds of natural pigments to cement, while its surface texture can be modified by the addition of sand or crushed marble. The tiles can also be decorated with designs and patterns using a sort of 'punch' into which different coloured mixtures are poured. There is no limit to the range of colours and designs that can be created in this way. Interlaced floral designs, Greek friezes, arabesques, checkerboard and diamond patterns are some of the long-standing favourites, while more modern designs are now being added to the repertoire. These miniature works of art have been given a new lease of life on the floors of many family homes and only need to acquire the patina which is built up over countless summer holidays.

Sitting rooms

'On the eve, that night
no one in the family idled:
they mulled wine [...].
The grandmother
worked her loom [...].
The mother was very
industrious; seated at
her ease, she sewed; Zine
sorted the saffron. The
men smoked pipes [...];
everyone in the inglenook
threw dried twigs.'

Théodore Aubanel

The idea of a 'sitting room' is not usually associated with the rustic dwellings of Provence. Until fairly recently, only country houses owned by wealthy city dwellers boasted the luxury of a room devoted to relaxation. Farmhouses simply had a main, communal room whose dimensions depended on the size of the *mas* and the number of servants who had to take their meals there. This room was used for socializing as well as for doing the chores and men and women would sometimes gather here for the evening. Everyone took turns to bring a candle or put oil in the lamp because these were the only means of lighting in country dwellings until the early 20th century. Describing the companionable gatherings of his childhood in his *Memoirs*, Nobel Prize-winning

Previous pages: The pale matt tones of Provençal sideboards and Gustavian chairs create a restful mood in a sitting room in the Luberon.
Above and right: The spacious living room of a house in northern Vaucluse boldly combines past and present. Plaster arches supported by beams create an undulating ceiling; Italian and Provençal furniture from the 18th and 19th centuries blends with the subdued colours and patinas. A grey stone rug has been laid over a cement floor.

Provençal writer Frédéric Mistral wrote that the candle had to last for two evenings. When it was half used, it was time to go to bed. As an economy measure, a grain of salt was placed next to the wick to make it burn slower. The lamps burned olive, almond or walnut oil and gave off a thick acrid smoke.

A completely different atmosphere reigned in the *mas* used as holiday homes by wealthy city dwellers. The decorative style of the mansions of Aix, Arles or Avignon was often imitated and reproduced. Lavish interiors offset the austere elegance of the architecture, making ample use of decorative features such as high ceilings, wood panelling and paintings.

There were some particularly fine examples of decorative plasterwork. In the 18th century, Italian artists working mainly in Provence began to replicate the large carved wood panels found in elegant city dwellings with sculpted plaster, generally left unpainted. Bas-reliefs, cartouches, trophies, mouldings and foliage reflected the decorative designs that were also found on local furniture. With truly southern flair, Provençal decorative arts created a fusion of three seemingly contradictory styles: Louis XIII, with its

Despite the imposing chandelier suspended 4.8m (16ft) above the floor, the impressive sitting room at the Château de Moissac looks very cosy. Linen sofas by Edith Mézard are sociably arranged around a table designed by Jacqueline Morabito, opposite a fireplace displaying a collection of ornamental jugs. Reproduction convent tables by Côté Bastide enclose this comfortable fireside area.

turned wood balusters, Louis XV, with its scalloped outlines and escargot feet, and Louis XVI. The wave of neo-classicism that swept France in the late 18th century did nothing to oust the earlier repertory of sinuous, graceful shapes. The urns and ewers of antiquity symbolized the home and family, while the acanthus leaf called to mind the gentle swell of the waves. Provençal furniture is largely made of carved, polished walnut: cupboards, *buffets à glissants* (dressers with sliding panels), chests of drawers and writing desks, generally with two large drawers. As well as the traditional chairs, a simple divan originated in Provence, called a *radassière*, from the Provençal word radassa, meaning 'to dawdle, laze about'. Inspired by the Turkish divan, this long seat is liberally scattered with cushions to make it more comfortable.

The fireplace, once the focal point of the main room, remained the centrepiece of the sitting room. Although occasionally made of plaster, the fireplace was usually built of stone and gave the mason an opportunity to show off his expertise. However this showpiece remained very simple: the projecting lintel, supported by rounded consoles, was decorated with a simple moulding also made of plaster and frequently adorned by a strip of gathered material, known locally as the *rabat-fumée*, a type of smoke-guard. Fireplaces with an enormous hood, as in *mas* in the Camargue, were described as *en alcôve* because, like the English inglenook fireplaces, they allowed several people to sit round the fire. In these cases, the lintel was either horizontal, cut from a single block of stone, or slightly arched and constructed of dressed stone.

Left: At the Domaine de Barbeiranne, in the Massif des Maures, the large windows of a sitting room designed as a winter garden by Bruno Lafourcade open onto an oak grove.
Above: The inviting coolness of an old converted barn, with two camp beds and a piece of bake-house furniture unearthed in L'Isle-sur-la-Sorgue, seems the perfect place to relax.
Following page: This sitting room-cum-library in the Var is a haven of peace.

In Ménerbes, the reception room of the Bastide de Marie (**above, facing page and p. 101**) is an attractive medley of greys; the sitting room is arranged into various relaxing areas with updated baroque chairs and a fine old bookcase. **Opposite left:** In a lush valley overlooking the Luberon, the sitting room of a welcoming house has a beautiful patinated bookcase, sofas by David Hicks and a low table made of stripped bamboo.

Straw-seated divans and wing chairs are traditional Provençal pieces of furniture. Although local craftsmen make fine reproductions, such as those by Bruno Carles (**above**), original pieces can be found in antique shops throughout Provence. **Bottom right:** A fine example spotted in the Mas de Curebourg, on L'Isle-sur-la-Sorgue.

Straw-seated chairs

Provençal traditions have always incorporated practices from elsewhere. Chairs are a typical example. The woven cord chairs that originated in Marseilles soon came to be called *chaises à la marseillaise* (Marseilles-chairs). These gave way to Italian style straw-seated chairs. The spread of this type of furniture throughout France from the 18th century onwards may well have started in Provence. The region, which is blessed with an abundance of straw and reeds, was obviously destined to make good use of these materials. The straw bottoms of the seats are made of sawwort, a triangulated marsh grass, that is wrapped in gold, green or red barley straw. A wider crosspiece, known as the *cache-paille*, is used to decorate the front of the chair and conceal the thickness of the straw. Provençal straw-seated chairs are renowned for their elaborate design, thanks to the expertise of the local joiners or *fustiers*. These craftsmen skilfully and tastefully interpreted forms inspired by Parisian cabinetwork. Between the days of the *ancien régime* (the old order of things before the 1789 revolution) and the 19th century, Provençal straw-seated chairs evolved. The more classic examples, influenced by Louis XVI style, are simply decorated with an oval tassel, also called an *olive*, on the two uprights of the back. Others, more elaborately decorated in Louis XV style, have violin-shaped backs, curved feet and a carved crosspiece at the front. This style was frequently reproduced during the 20th century, but there are countless different types of Provençal chairs: low craftsmen's or hearth chairs, *bonne femme* or *capucine* chairs, as well as many sofas, often rather incorrectly called *radassiers*, which feature prominently in many hallways.

Dining rooms

' In that penumbra, one
could make out the pétrin
(kneading trough) in
black wood, shaped like a
sarcophagus, with carved
swords and flowers,
and surmounted by its
openwork basket with
Moorish pinnacles, where
bread was kept fresh in
all Provençal farmhouses.'

ALPHONSE DAUDET

Only larger houses had a separate dining room and kitchen. In the more humble *mas*, a long walnut table polished by generations of elbows dominated the centre of the room. The straw-seated chairs around it were made with rye straw in natural colours. A low sideboard with two folding doors was generally the only other piece of furniture. The dining room might also sport another finely carved piece, a narrow, fairly low dresser called a *glissant*, recognizable by sliding panels on either side of a central door called the *tabernacle*. A more opulent house might contain fine corner cup-boards for crockery and other necessities, either an elbow-high cupboard or two, one on top of the other. Their elegant rounded frontage, decorated with moulded panels, has the advantage of taking up less room than a rectangular dresser. Provençal cuisine is not only distinctive for its unique blend

of flavours, but because it uses certain pieces of furniture and utensils found nowhere else. Many houses gave pride of place to some of the most original Provençal designs, such as the *blutoir* (sifting machine), the *pétrin* (kneading trough), the *panetière* (bread chest), the *boîte à sel* (salt box) and the *farinière* (flour box – into which food was dipped, before frying). There was also the tin, copper or faience fountain with its basin. These objects and pieces of furniture, now very rare and valuable, have made their way into the dining room. In bygone days, the men used to eat their meals first, while the women ate standing near the fireplace the better to serve their menfolk, as can be seen in the film *Angèle* by Marcel Pagnol, based on a short story by Jean Giono (1934). In one scene, the head of the household lunches with his simple-minded farmhand, played by Fernandel, both being served by the mistress of the house. Fortunately, the days of such power plays are over and mealtimes are now much more sociable gatherings.

Previous pages: The small dining room in the Château Val-Joanis is flanked by painted wood-panelled cupboards and, in traditional Provençal style, the table is set with three tablecloths laid on top of each other.
Top left: In the charming dining room at the Château de l'Ange, the splendidly long table (M. Biehn) and Edith Mézard's linen-covered garden chairs stand on a floor of reclaimed flagstones.
Opposite: A Var dining room in the Venetian spirit, created by Maurice Savinel and Roland Le Bévillon, with a trompe-l'oeil dresser between two mesh-fronted cupboards.

Religious festivals were the occasion for formal dinners. On Christmas Eve, the table was ceremonially covered with three tablecloths, each laid on top of the other, corresponding to the three festivals of the Nativity, the Circumcision and the Epiphany. Three candles were lit in honour of the Holy Trinity. It was a bad omen if the wick of one of the candles bent towards a guest, as the number three was thought to bring bad luck: according to an old proverb, '*Tres, la mort l'es*' ('three means death'). The table remained laid for the duration of the festivals. The corners of the tablecloths were lifted to keep the crumbs safe as, during the night, they provided sustenance for ancestors' spirits.

The Christmas tradition of the *gros souper* (big supper) is still kept alive in Provence. Contrary to what its name suggests, this is a light meal eaten before midnight Mass. All the dishes for this special yet simple meal are served at the same time, traditional main courses and desserts being put on the table in a spectacular display of abundance before the guests take their seats. This mode of presentation, customary in the poorest of houses as well as in the wealthiest, recalls the aristocratic 'French-style service' of pre-Revolutionary France, when all the dishes were presented to the guests at the same time.

Previous pages, left: In a superb house in Carpentras, the antiques dealer Jean-Jacques Bourgeois has devised an attractive eating area, juxtaposing an antique birdcage with furniture by Vincent Mit l'Ane, L'Isle-sur-la-Sorgue.
Right: Interior designer Estelle Réale covers the table with Souleiado fabrics, and adds an old grocery cupboard, discovered at G. Nicod, L'Isle-sur-la-Sorgue, and some chestnut-wood armchairs.

Left: In the Mas de Curebourg, on the hills of Villeneuve-lès-Avignon, L'Isle-sur-la-Sorgue, a dresser displays a varied collection.
Above: Interior designer France Loeb used antique sheets for the blinds, table and chairs in this elegant dining room; the 18th-century cupboard reputedly comes from the outbuildings at Versailles.
Left: A monastic atmosphere prevails in the vaulted dining room at the Bastide de Marie where a zinc-covered dining table is surrounded by Provence & Fils chairs.

A menu described by Lanery d'Arc in 1894 could, with just a few variations, apply to a meal prepared today: 'Here are the raw celery hearts that have been whitening for months in the soil and that are eaten with anchovy fillets softened in olive oil in a sauceboat before the fire; here is the "*muge en riste*" (mullet) glistening in its thick red sauce scattered with olives; cod, fried or in a cream sauce, dark, melting "*carde*" (chard), gratin of herbs or "*tian*", spinach stuffed with clams and mussels under a crusty layer of cheese, and the large eel, spit-roasted like a chicken.' There were thirteen desserts, in memory of Christ and his twelve apostles, as well as figs, nuts, almonds, raisins, apples

and fresh grapes stored since autumn, honey and jam, and above all black and white nougat, often home-made, not forgetting the *pompe*, a traditional loaf flavoured with olive oil or perfumed with orange-flower and generously sprinkled with sugar. 'The mixture goes into the baker's oven and emerges covered in bumps and golden as the breastplate of Bradamante [heroine of Ariosto's *Orlando Furioso*], smelling exquisite. [...] Not modestly exquisite like the smell of mignonette, but violently and extravagantly exquisite', enthused Giono. Oil, flour and sugar are all that are needed to work such miracles. These simple living traditions encapsulate the spirit of Provence.

Previous pages: A table set for a festive dinner under the vaulted ceiling of a mas in Grasse (left). In the Château de Gignac, designer Michèle Joubert has retained the tradition of dining beside the original 18th-century fireplace, over which hangs a late 19th-century mirror from the Mas de Curebourg (right).
Right: In the Château de Moissac, a homely breakfast table, covered with a simple hemp tablecloth.
Above: A buffet à glissant (dresser) in the Musée Arlaten.

Earthenware

Two of the largest and most famous earthenware factories of the *ancien régime* were based in Provence, in Moustiers and Marseilles. Moustiers is traditionally held to be the birthplace of French faience, or tin-glazed earthenware, introduced by Pierre Clérissy, a potter who is said to have been taught the technique in 1660 by an Italian monk from Faenza, where it originated. Provence was already renowned for the fine quality of its different clays, which were carefully selected and left to decompose in cellars to improve their malleability. In the space of twenty or thirty years, Moustiers became a leading producer of prestigious pottery. The most sought-after styles of decoration were the large *lambrequins* (scallops) in the light, elegant style of Jean Bérain (architect and ornamental decorator), which echoed the stately movements of minuets at the court of Louis XIV. Plates with scalloped or wavy edges and helmet-shaped ewers took their inspiration from the silver tableware they replaced when the ruinously expensive wars of the Sun King made it necessary to melt down silverware. The names that made the Moustiers faience industry famous abound: Viry, Olérys and Laugier, Fouque and Pelloquin, the Ferrat brothers, Féraud and Berbégier. They supplied all the major courts of Europe and formed an elite that was admired throughout southern France. However, they were hit hard by the fashion for fine English porcelain and china and, in the middle of the 19th century, the Moustiers workshops closed one after the other. The industry ground to a halt between 1874 and 1928, until Marcel Provence relighted a kiln. Moustiers swiftly regained its former prosperity, becoming what some regard as the capital of the Provençal crafts industry.

An embarrassment of riches from
Provence including 19th-century
slipware (**above**), traditional Louis
XV-style plates by Foucard-Jourdan,
at Vallauris (**top right**), elaborate
tureens made from a mixture of clays
(**below**) and a 19th-century scalloped
Apt faience dish at the Musée Souleiado
in Tarascon (**right**).

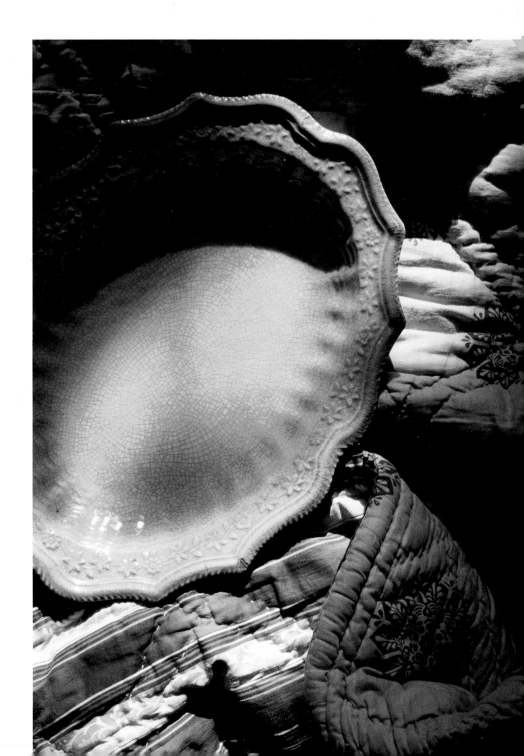

After it has been washed, filtered and had its impurities removed, the clay is left to stand in plaster bowls in the Bernard factory, Apt (**top**). The subtle colours of the different types of clay create a design that runs through the paste (**below**), which is then made into sweet-boxes decorated with naturally shaped leaves and handmade flowers (**left**).
Right: Gazpacho served in tians or shallow earthenware dishes from Terre et Provence.

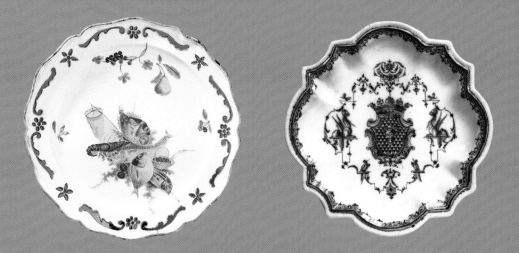

No such recovery was in store for Marseilles after the crisis caused by competition across the channel. However, the memory of the Veuve Perrin factory is still very much alive. It had made its name with the extremely naturalistic decorations of '*fleurs jetées*' (scattered flowers). These small motifs originally concealed tiny blemishes in the paste, the decoration being executed freehand on the enamel after the first firing. Marseilles wares were notable for the variety of colours achieved through exceptional mastery of the techniques of the second and third firing. The factories used not only the traditional sharp fire method but also the more subtle method of mild firing, which enabled them to produce a greater variety of colours. Marseilles ceramics are also admired for their consummate use of coloured glazes. These sulphur-based glazes are beautifully translucent. Connoisseurs also value the work of other factories that were just as sophisticated, if less prestigious, such as the faienceries of Apt, which eschewed the complex 18th-century models for the delicate effects achieved by the famous marbled pottery, produced by means of the so-called 'nougatine' technique. This involved mixing different clays whose colours varied owing to the metal oxides they contained.

Although these treasures may seem too valuable for use in holiday homes, they are a lesson in local history, recalling the noble origins of the *mas* or *bastides* and symbolizing all the refinement and grace of these traditional dwellings.

Kitchens

'The big hare was waiting
on an earthenware plate.
[...] Honoré had packed
it with a stuffing in the
style of his own region,
doing something magical
with fresh herbs from
the garden and from
the mountain.'

JEAN GIONO

Apart from the bedrooms, traditional rural dwellings in Provence boasted only one other room. Used as a kitchen, dining room and a place where family and friends could gather, it embodied the legendary hospitality of the region. The kitchen is the successor to this communal room. It is the 'hearth' both figuratively and literally, because it is often the only room in the house with a fireplace. In the early 20th century, the stove was generally unknown in the *mas*: food was cooked on a spit or in a large pot over the fire in the hearth, which had what was known as a *crémascle* or trammel and large andirons, whose upper section supported

Previous pages: A warm shade of yellow and antique glazed tiles from Aubagne. The 19th-century iron table is surrounded by Provençal chairs; the floor is covered with reclaimed flagstones.
Above: A yellow marble table and worktop for this country kitchen with its collection of antique pottery and small 19th-century landscapes.
Right: this sunny kitchen near Tarascon displays rows of enamel saucepans, lids and jars of spices.

This kitchen in the Var (**above**) has been designed
by Maurice Savinel and Roland Le Bévillon to give
a view of the garden through the adjoining dining
room. The hood was modelled on that of the
Château d'Entrecasteaux, the walnut units with
their pietra serena worktop resemble an antique
pharmacy cupboard and, prominent in the centre,
is an island unit with basket drawers by Henri
Quinta for Campagne Première. A traditional
Provençal kitchen by the same designers (**opposite**)
has been given a touch of Venetian style. The hood
is faced with tiles from Alain Vagh in Salernes and
the worktop is marble; the butchers' block came
from the second-hand market in Cogolin.

the bowl of broth or tea. Frequently found beneath the same vast hood, the *potager* was a type of large cooking range indispensable for cooking over the embers. Made of masonry and topped with ceramic tiles, it could not compete with modern conveniences and was often replaced by a wood-burning stove, itself ousted by the gas cooker. Next to the fireplace stood the sink, whose water was sometimes supplied by a tank. There was no draining board for preparing food, but several alcoves and cupboards for storing everyday products and crockery; saucepans were hung on the wall, and cooking pots and numerous ceramic dishes were arranged on shelves. In addition, there was the larder, a cramped little room lit by a small north-facing window, which was used to keep delicate foodstuffs cool.

In a mas in the Gard (above), the architect Pierre Cossonnet has fitted a kitchen into the same space as the living room and the dining room, beneath the arched stone ceiling of the former barn. This welcoming area is designed around a masonry island that is topped with earthenware tiles and used to conceal crockery and appliances. A country kitchen in the foothills of Mont Ventoux (opposite) smells deliciously of local produce. Under the zinc worktop, patinated oak cupboards conceal the household appliances.

The only objects adorning the walls were religious prints, a jam-making pan, several utensils and a rack of hunting guns. Alphonse Daudet's description of Valmajour is a perfect illustration of this type of room: 'Two or three devout pictures, Saints Mary and Martha and La Tarasque [a legendary monster from Tarascon], the small antique-looking copper lamp hanging from a fine whitewood ring carved by a shepherd, the salt box and flour box on either side of the fireplace completed the decoration of this vast room along with a conch shell, used for calling the beasts, that gleamed above the mantelpiece of the hearth. The long table extended the length of the room and was

flanked by benches and stools. Strings of onions hung from the ceiling, black with flies that buzzed every time the door curtain was raised.'

Nowadays, wickerwork objects, glazed earthenware utensils and rustic furniture like the *tamisadou*, a large sideboard concealing a metal cylinder operated by a handle, that was used to sift wheat, are mainly displayed simply for their decorative appearance.

*In the Château Barbeiranne, near Hyères (**left**), wine is sampled under the vaulted ceiling of the former sheepfold, now the kitchen. The worktop is covered with Alain Vagh tiles.*

Above: *A 19th-century marble potager (range) from Xavier Nicod, L'Isle-sur-la-Sorgue sets the tone for the new kitchens at the Château de Gignac, where interior designer Michèle Joubert has mingled flea-market finds, a La Cornue cooker and a stone floor (Chabaud, in Apt).*

Opposite, left: At the foot of the Palais des Papes, delicious smells waft from a cookery class at the Hôtel La Mirande. The leading chefs of the region run 'Le Marmiton' (the Kitchen Boy), a cookery school offering practical courses open to all. The former kitchens of the 19th-century mansion have been reworked and redecorated by Martin Stein. The kitchen units in lime green wood were made by the Reynier firm in Carpentras, the marble worktops by Leydier in Avignon, and the walls are covered with reclaimed faience tiles from a Marseilles café.

Opposite, right: At the Château Val-Joanis, in the Luberon, the former granary has been converted into a kitchen. The fireplace, windows, cornice, shelves and cupboards are built into the thick wall; the glossy red Aubagne tiles on the wall came from the former dovecotes and the painted wooden furniture was made to measure. The worktop and the sink are made of Brignoles stone and the Louis XIII-style chairs around the large oak table are covered with loose covers in Canovas fabric.

Following pages: The best find in this Vaucluse kitchen, furnished piecemeal from trips to flea-markets, has to be the marble sink with its wavy sides, resembling a tian, *discovered at Saint-Cannat. It is fixed on top of some antique cupboards and flanked with marble worktops and a back wall covered with English Victorian tiles, themselves surmounted by a scalloped wooden shelf that echoes the shape of the sink. The original hood shelters the house's old stove and a Godin cooker linked by a decorative marble panel.*

Page 134: In Martine de Fontanes' Maison d'Uzès, the kitchen larder is crowded with everyday ceramics and period Provençal pitchers.

Page 135: An entirely remodelled kitchen in Saint-Rémy-de-Provence displays worktops made of glazed tiles from Salernes. Vegetables and lettuce from the garden wait to be washed in the marble sink.

Opposite: The 'Bastide' kitchen, designed by De Tonge, takes its colours from the soil around Roussillon. The dresser with sliding doors, the worktops and the sink made of distressed, polished stone form an attractive contrast to the solid oak butcher's block and table.

Piles and gatouilles

The stone pile (pilo in Provençal), used as a drinking trough and even, sometimes, as a washtub, was situated in the courtyard, near the well. Inside the house, the sink (eiguié) was sometimes placed near the fireplace and sometimes in the gatouille, *a lean-to next to the main room. When there was no inside sink, a water-bucket was kept in the room at all times. Although in most of Provence the sink was usually of stone, a small, deep, glazed terracotta sink called a* tian *was sometimes made by craftsmen in Salernes, the centre of ceramic production in the Haut-Var. These old installations can still give good service, if connected to running water.*

At the Forge d'Opio, pitchers, oil and vinegar bottles and earthenware jars by Denise Garnier (**left**) display typical southern colours in rows on the shelves.
Below: Green flower-shaped plates from the Louis XV service by Foucard-Jourdan in Vallauris, with a fruit plate and a small leaf-shaped dish in a lighter shade of green.
Right, top: Shallow marbled bowls, a deep red egg dish by Foucard-Jourdan, and a late 19th-century earthenware terrine.
Below: In Vallauris, the elegant simplicity of freshly glazed dishes of the late 19th century or early 20th century.

Household pottery

Earthenware is a thriving industry in Provence since all the pottery of the region is made from it. Glassware is usually reserved for special occasions, although it may be used every day in grand, wealthy houses. Known locally as *terraio*, this pottery is arranged on a shelf hung from the wall, called the *esudelié*, in the main room of old farmhouses. Vallauris has specialized in the manufacture of earthenware since the Gallo-Roman period, but the influx of Genoese potters in the 16th century gave a fresh boost to this craft industry. The manufacturing process is well known: the clays are first mixed with water, then filtered. The paste is then dried and degassed to remove the air bubbles that would ruin the firing. After coating with slip, the piece is fired for the first time at over 1,000°C (1,832°F) in an electric kiln. The 'biscuit clay' body that emerges is then dipped and glazed on the inside, before being fired again, at a slightly lower temperature, also in an electric kiln. The last wood-burning kiln at Vallauris was extinguished in 1938. Many other villages have acquired a reputation for the production of fine earthenware, including Valbonne, Opio, Levens, Gréollières, Cliouscat, Aigues-Vives and Saint-Quentin-la-Poterie. Although many basic shapes are produced, two designs are typical of Provence: the *pignate*, a cylindrical cooking-pot superseded in the industrial era by the cast-iron casserole dish, and the *douire* or *bombouno*, a large oil jar with several pairs of handles. In Arles, this jar was also called a '*conscience*' or a '*gueux*' (beggar), because it contained the oil that was given to the poor.

Bedrooms

'This time it's my bedroom. […] The walls are a pale violet. The floor is of red tiles. The wood of the bed and the chairs is the yellow of fresh butter, the sheet and the pillowcases are clear lemon yellow. The coverlet is bright red. […] And that's all – there's nothing in this room with closed shutters.'

VINCENT VAN GOGH

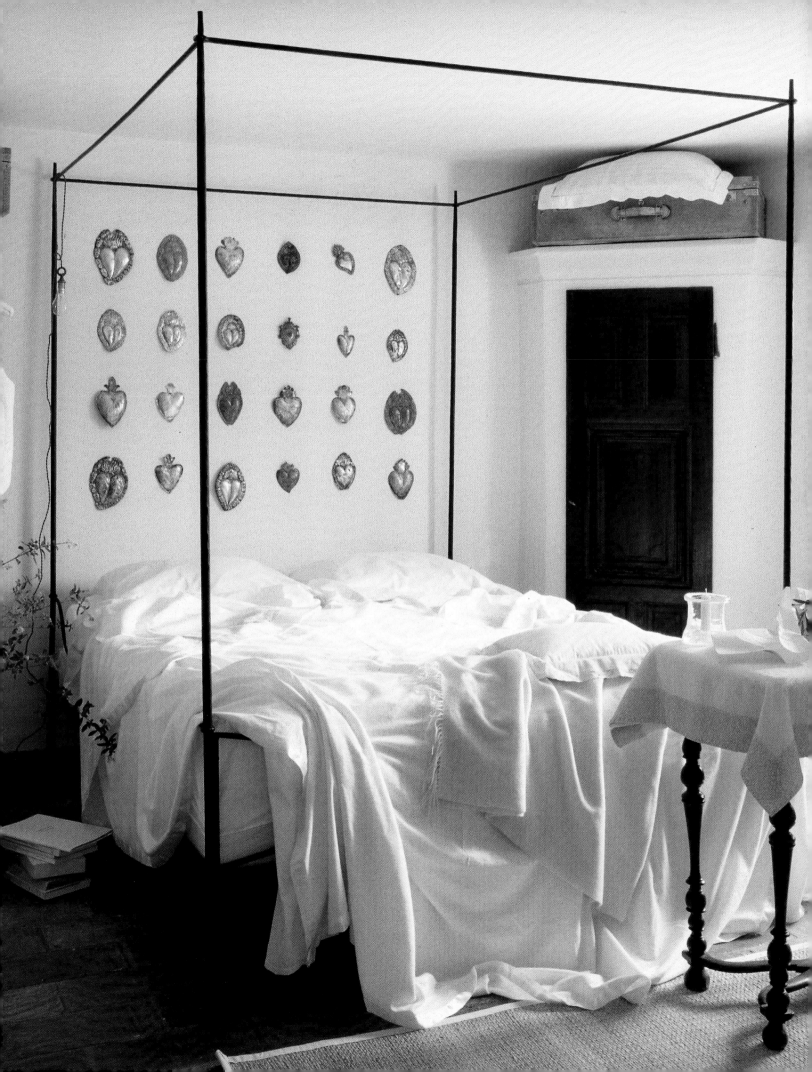

Previous pages: Simple touches for a beautiful bedroom designed by Jacqueline Morabito: wrought-iron adds a hint of glamour to a monastic bed, while the textures of the cotton and linen lighten the mood.

Opposite, left: A creamy glow envelops this farmhouse bedroom in the foothills of Mont Ventoux. The 18th-century bed is covered with sheets designed by Edith Mézard.

Above: A stunning 19th-century Neapolitan bed, painted and patinated by Jacqueline Morabito.

Right: This bedroom pays tribute to the 18th century with a superb toile de Jouy *print on a Louis XVI bed and a straw-seated chair.*

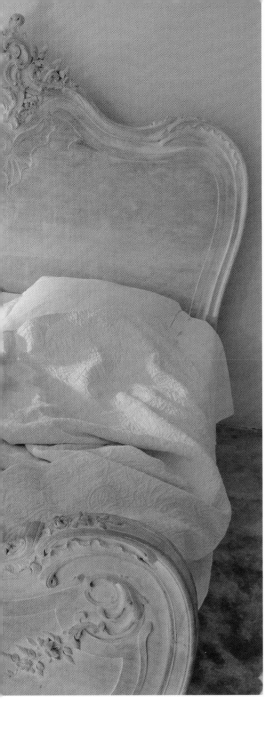

In most old Provençal farm-houses, the bedrooms are located upstairs, next to the corn loft. These small rooms are rarely more than ten square metres (108 sq. ft) in area. In poorer dwellings, parents and young children slept together. Many families supplemented their income with a silkworm farm, and when a house had no silkworm nursery wooden racks containing the silkworms were sometimes put in the bedroom, particularly during the critical hatching stage, since the valuable silkworms cannot tolerate the cold. The family then moved temporarily into the loft or the barn. This was not considered an ordeal, since what was solemnly called the 'education' of the silkworm represented a crucial source of income until the early 20th century.

'We'll hear nothing, for miles and miles, except cicadas.'

COLETTE

In the more affluent houses of Provence and other regions, husbands and wives slept in separate bedrooms. There was one exception to this rule: in Provence, guests are traditionally offered the best bedroom, generally that used by the head of the household, who then doubled-up with his wife.

Traditionally, the bedrooms were very simply decorated, with a terracotta floor and whitewashed walls, as in the main room. Two pieces of furniture vied for attention, at least in terms of size: the wardrobe and the bed. The bed (*litocho*) was usually a plain solid wood bedstead, sometimes adorned with a decoratively shaped and elaborately carved bedhead and, at the foot, two carved posts linked by a crosspiece

ornamented with the usual motifs of prosperity and fertility. It was spread with a quilted *boutis* coverlet; a bedside rug on the floor made getting up in the morning slightly less daunting. A bull hide often served as a bedside floor covering in the *mas* of the Camargue.

Often bedrooms did not even have a fireplace. The tiny room in Arles occupied by Vincent Van Gogh, which he painted in 1889 (in the Musée d'Orsay, in Paris), is proof of this rural simplicity. Two straw-seated chairs, a small table with a pitcher and bowl for washing, a mirror framed with dark wood and a simple bed stand out against the light blue of the walls.

Above: In the Château de l'Ange, an embroidered linen cover by Edith Mézard is tied over a striped linen bedhead and co-ordinated with a topstitched bedspread.
Right: Also in the Luberon, a crystal pendant chandelier hangs from the original beams, which have been simply whitewashed. A cheesecloth mosquito net has been hung to serve as a canopy and mosquito net and the bed is covered by an antique boutis bedspread.

The moulded doors are painted a darker contrasting blue. The only luxuries in this bedroom are the artist's paintings, hung above the bed.

The bedroom walls were more commonly adorned with small objects that are generally associated with Provençal interiors, such as *bénitiers* (fonts). These come in all shapes and materials: tin with an openwork design, glazed earthenware and even spun glass. Brightly coloured religious images, alphabet primers cross-stitched by well-behaved little girls and small pictures made of multicoloured glass beads are typical Provençal touches. These sparkling images were

Near Saint-Rémy-de-Provence, this refined bedroom (above) is encircled by a frieze of olive leaves. A large mirror stands directly on the floor. The bed is covered with cotton sheets by Edith Mézard and the table is spread with voluminous quilted boutis. In a village in northern Vaucluse (right), this bedroom is a haven of peace with its floor of faded red hexagonal tiles and furniture by Vivement Jeudi, in Paris.

found in abundance at the famous fair at Beaucaire, as were plaster *santibelli*, popular devotional pieces that served as decorative objects, now keenly sought after by collectors. A glass bell protects their dazzling colours and gilding from dust and marks: Virgin and child surrounded by lilies, martyred saints crowned with flowers holding a gilt paper palm leaf. Produced in Naples and Sicily, these statuettes were sold in Provence by Italian peddlers who used to cry: 'Santi belli! Santi belli!' (beautiful saints). They were copied by Provençal craftsmen, although their statuettes, known as *santons*, were made of terracotta instead of plaster and resembled large crib figurines.

Left: The dazzling whitewash gives this room an aura of sophistication enhanced by the twin beds spread with heavy embroidered linen-cotton covers (Maison de Vacances) and a Blanc d'Ivoire ecru boutis bedspread. The attics of the Château de Moissac in the Haut-Var (above) have been converted into three interconnecting bedrooms limewashed in varying shades by craftsman Marcel Rossi. In the midday sunshine, the chandelier casts flashes of light onto the painted iron bed.

Above: the peaceful blue-green
bedroom in the Bastide de Marie,
in Ménerbes, looks inviting with its
Provence & Fils bed under a filmy
organdie mosquito net: a tasteful
reinterpretation of old Provence.
A low wall cleverly conceals the
bathroom area, decorated in subtle
matching shades.

A cabinet to last a lifetime

Walnut was the material of choice for traditional Provençal furniture. Its fine grain and warm, rich colour, deepening with the patina of age, accentuates the elegant mouldings and the animated carving. Placed in a prominent position in the bedrooms of large houses, the wedding wardrobe formed part of the bride's dowry and contained her trousseau: all the linen she would use throughout her life and even afterwards since one of the sheets in the trousseau would eventually serve as a shroud. This tradition, which betrays a certain familiarity with death, persisted until the early 20th century. The doors of the wardrobe were carved with symbols intended to ensure the young couple's happiness and prosperity: a quiver and arrows, the attributes of love, and symbols of plenty such as pearl necklaces or baskets of flowers (sometimes substituted with a soup tureen). These cabinets also display the work of excellent wrought-iron craftsmen, the generous hinges being virtuoso feats of engineering, as were the open-work locks that extended the entire length of the doors.

Left, bottom: At La Bastide, a guest house in Saint-Martin-de-Crau, an air of serenity imbues this spotless room where a basket doubles as a crib.
Above: Detail of a carved monogram within a medallion on a fine Provençal cabinet at the Musée Arlaten.

Patchworks, quilts and printed calico

Formerly kept carefully folded away in the depths of vast cupboards, printed fabrics, quilted skirts and *boutis* coverlets now enliven the simplest of houses with their fresh, bright colours. The vogue for these traditional fabrics over the last few years has made them a popular choice for decorating Provençal homes. Quality reproductions can be used instead of antique fabrics, which are now rare and very fragile.

Eighteenth-century inventories show that a number of wealthy houses in Marseilles and the surrounding areas were decorated with painted cotton fabrics, known locally as *tapisseries de Marseille* ('Marseilles tapestries'). Although none of these delicate hangings survive today, the printed fabrics that have been a Provençal speciality since the 17th century can be used to similar effect. These materials, painted or printed, with shimmering colours and an infinite variety of motifs, were inspired by cottons imported from India that were block-printed with lush floral patterns, multicoloured birds and fantastic fruits. India had mastered the art of fixing colours long before, and these precious fabrics, arriving in Provence as a result of the trade between Marseilles and the ports of the Levant, were soon imitated. Being a region rich in mineral colours, Provence proved particularly favourable for the cultivation of plants used to make dye. Some even grew there naturally, like the dyer's broom of Mont Ventoux, which produced a deep yellow. Woad and indigo from the Orient were used to make blue, while red was obtained from the root of the madder, which was dried then left to ferment in barrels. Known since

These two examples illustrate the difference between boutis and piqué fabrics.
Above: *A piqué bedspread, known locally as* peso sus peso *or patchwork, made from different pieces of silk.*
Below: *A bedspread made from two embroidered boutis skirts in Avignon taffeta dating from 1770.*
Right: *a Provençal armchair covered with printed calico (Les Olivades).*

Above: 19th-century piqué skirts from Arles, Marseilles and the Comtat-Venaissin. At the Musée Souleiado in Tarascon **(left and below)**, piqué counterpanes with petit point embroidery, a superb collection of 18th- and 19th-century coverlets and an engraved printing block made of fruit wood. *Right:* shelves stacked with *boutis* and piqué coverlets at the Maison Biehn and some early 20th-century Provençal skirts thrown carelessly onto a chair.

earliest historical times (it produced the celebrated *rouge d'Andrinople*, a deep red), the madder plant was introduced into the Comtat-Venaissin (the present *département* of Vaucluse) during the 18th century. Marseilles and Avignon became such large production centres of these *Indiennes* (printed calicos) that they became a cause for concern for their textile rivals, Nîmes and Lyons. The technique of printing with engraved wooden blocks (one block being used for each colour) is now employed only in a handful of craft studios or for special orders. From the late 18th century, it was gradually replaced by the technique of printing with copper rollers. These fabrics were used not only for decoration and furnishings such as wall hangings, curtains, chair coverings and counterpanes but also for women's clothing. Often combined with Marseilles piqué embroidery, printed calicos are just as popular today. Subtle combinations of different colours and motifs in the same room can be highly effective. Stylish Provençals of the 18th and 19th centuries, particularly the women from Arles, first set the trend by boldly mixing and matching various printed, sewn, embroidered or quilted materials in their traditional costume.

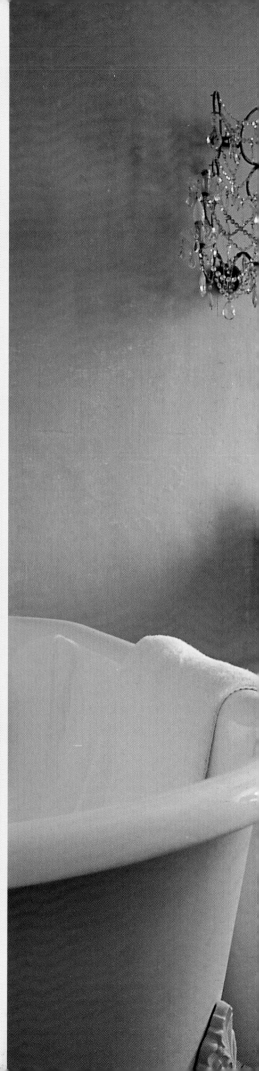

Bathrooms and linen rooms

'[…] when full summer arrived, she blocked the Gaudissard stream with branches and mud and laid a sheet down in the bottom of the stream […]. This made a big, clean basin. And she bathed in it. She washed herself from top to bottom with a fistful of soapwort.'

JEAN GIONO

The first proper bathrooms to appear on the Côte d'Azur were in the luxury hotels built in Nice or Cannes to accommodate Victorian tourists from England. Winter holiday makers, accustomed to running water in the spa hotels of Vichy and Vittel, wanted to enjoy the same ultramodern facilities in their rooms. Most of these luxury hotel bathrooms, with their white faience-tiled walls, large spotless porcelain washbasins, monumental claw-foot bathtubs and nickel-plated taps, disappeared when these establishments were modernized one after the other.

At this time, the typical Provençal house had no actual bathroom. The ritual of Roman-style bathing was a distant memory in Provence, as it was in all the Latin countries. While thermal facilities, as described by

Previous pages: A bathroom at the Château de Moissac contains an antique washbasin, period Venetian wall-lights and an old door re-hung as a corner cupboard.
Opposite: Shutters separate a bedroom from this bathroom which has an antique basin set into a draper's table from Nicod, L'Isle-sur-la-Sorgue.
Right: At the Bastide de Marie, in Ménerbes, two simple Philippe Starck basins rest on a stone surface.
Bottom: An antique bathtub encircled by a frieze.

Titus Livius, Pliny the Elder or Plutarch, who made particular mention of the hot springs at Aix or Digne, remained available in spas frequented for health reasons, a fairly rudimentary daily wash was deemed sufficient in pre-Revolutionary France. From the late Middle Ages on, people distrusted water, believing it to be responsible for spreading all types of epidemics and public baths had a bad reputation. People preferred to wash in the farmhouse kitchen or have a quick morning sluice in a basin on a washstand in the bedroom, which was sometimes hidden behind a screen. Many paintings by artists who regularly visited the South of France in the late 19th century or early 20th century depict intimate scenes of women bathing, stooping over a porcelain basin or sitting in a tub in the middle of a bedroom. It was not until 1925 that Pierre Bonnard, for example, showed his magnificent nudes bathing in a bathtub.

'The linen was put in place, clean, folded, mended, and filled with lavender flowers.'

Henri Bosco

Some homeowners treat their bathrooms as a boudoir in the aristocratic style of an 18th-century *bastide*. Conversely, in a fairly recent development, bathrooms are now sometimes designed to open onto the bedroom. Whatever the choice of materials or style, antique mirrors or basins made of glazed cement, mosaic lanterns or frosted glass washbasins, there seem to be three key elements of the southern bathroom: coolness, light and tranquillity. How these qualities are achieved in keeping with the style of the house is a matter of individual choice.

*The bath in the white bedroom in the Bastide de Moustiers (**above**) is softened with a ceramic fresco from the Atelier Soleil in Moustiers, and concealed behind white curtains. A comfortable Indonesian armchair beckons.*
***Right:** At the Hôtel Le Mas de Peint, in Camargue, interior designer Estelle Réale has designed a bathtub with a canopy formed by two linen curtains lined with waterproof fabric.*

Linen rooms and bugadières

Any bastide *worthy of the name has a small room adjacent to the main room; when used exclusively for laundry, it is called the* bugado *or* bugadière. *Here linen was sorted into piles, for washing in the tub, washing in cold water or the pile reserved for the grand annual wash. When the time for the annual wash came round, the communal room took on the appearance of a battleground, much to the children's delight. The laundry was bundled up in old sheets then covered with cinders; boiling water was poured over them to produce steam and the lot was left to soak. Lavender oil was added to the final rinse, imbuing the laundry with an enduring scent.*

Previous pages: In this washroom at the Château Sainte Roseline in the Var (**left**), *troughs have been carved from pale gold Portuguese* calizza capri *stone. At the La Ribaude guest house in the Vaucluse* (**right**), *the morning sun streams into a bathroom where the sturdy tub is flanked by two Duravit washbasins.*

Above: *A bow-tied curtain gives a touch of charm to a practical linen room.*
Left: *A cupboard smelling sweetly of freshly starched linen*
Opposite: *a spacious, light-filled laundry.*

Small blocks with rough-cut edges, 300g (just over 1/2lb) oblong cakes, traditional large slabs or bars wrapped in Kraft paper and tied with string or raffia for sophisticated tastes: real Marseilles soap uses the most natural ingredients. It was formerly made in pretty moulds (**below**) and inspired some stylish posters.

Marseilles soap

According to Pliny the Elder, the Gauls invented soap, a basic mixture of wood ashes and goat tallow. However, it was the Arabs who perfected the formula based on olive oil and soda that is still in use today. In the Middle Ages, Marseilles had several prosperous soap-making factories and a 1688 decree by Colbert gave a further boost to this industry. Today, a handful of families still keep this tradition alive.

The process is simple: oil is heated and gradually becomes a paste on contact with the soda: this is known as the first change. After cooking for about twelve hours, the process of saponification is complete. The paste is then washed in cold water and stirred in a kettle to remove all impurities and traces of soda. After this, it is poured into vast cement vats called *mises* (frame moulds). The surface is then levelled with a metal utensil known as an *arable*. Once it has cooled and solidified, the paste is cut into large rectangular blocks. Each block is then machine-cut again by steel wires: the gleaming amber cubes of soap obtained in this fashion are left to dry on wire racks for several weeks. They may then be stamped with the manufacturers' brand name. The colour of the soap depends on the type of oil used. Olive oil produces a pretty green soap. Pale gold soaps are made with exotic oils that have been imported to Marseilles for generations: copra, palm, groundnut, etc. The soap-maker often creates skilful blends, depending on the individual properties of each oil. No longer used in laundries since the advent of the washing machine, Marseilles soap is now renowned for its eco-friendly qualities. Although still used for hand washing delicate garments, it is now making a triumphant comeback in elegant bathrooms, perfumed with a few drops of aromatic oil.

Acknowledgements

The editor would like to offer her heartfelt thanks to the editorial team
at Maisons Côté Sud and, in particular, to Françoise Lefébure, for her
knowledge and her unfailing passion for Provence, to Catherine Peyre,
who compiled most of the captions, and to Suzanne Lapauze, for her
efficiency, availability and her good humour.

We would also like to thank Christelle Fucili, Stéphanie Mastronicola
and Alice Harang for their invaluable contribution.

Stylists

Joëlle Balaresque H.-D.: p. 89 botton left, 127 bottom, 140 left. Marie-Hélène Balivet: p. 51 top. Laurence Botta: p. 6 left and right, 19 bottom, 25, 33, 34 top right 39 bottom, 44, 49, 57, 58, 63, 73 left, 83, 85 bottom, 109, 119 bottom right, 126, 127 top, 131 bottom, 152, 163 bottom. Sabine Bouvet: p. 4, 153 left. Milù Cachat: p. 29 left, 52 bottom left, 99, 121, 144, 146, 161. Marie-Christine Caviglione: p. 7 left and centre, 42, 73 right, 87 right, 96-97, 98, 112, 117, 128, 129, 136 right, 137, 138-139, 147, 154-155, 162. Julie Daurel: p. 38, 51 bottom right. Geneviève Dortignac: p. 91. Monique Duveau: p. 71, 92-93, 135 right, 143, 159. Brigitte Forgeur: p. 153 right. Muriel Gauthier: p. 35, 45 right, 67 bottom, 72, 100, 158. Caroline Guiol: p. 66 bottom left, 88, 89 top, 89 bottom right. Hélène Lafforgue: p. 6 centre, 12, 14-15, 16, 17, 19 top, 20, 23, 28, 31 bottom, 32, 39 top, 43, 60, 62 right, 68-69, 82 right, 84, 90 left, 94, 95, 103 bottom, 104 bottom left, 105, 111, 113 right, 119 top left, 124, 125, 132-133, 135 left, 145, 156, 157 bottom. Françoise Lefébure: p. 8, 24 bottom right, 40, 41, 48, 54-55, 61, 66 bottom right, 70 left, 74, 75, 76 bottom left, 82 left, 85 top, 87 left, 101, 102, 103 top, 104 top, 160-107, 108, 110, 113 left, 119 top right, 131 top, 141, 148 top, 157 top. Christine Lippens: p. 160. Jacqueline Morabito: p. 13 bottom, 21, 31 top, 59, 70 right, 86, 114, 115, 122-123, 130, 140 centre, 142, 151 top, 151 bottom left, 163 top. Chris O'Byrne: p. 11, 26-27, 30, 56, 76 top, 77, 78, 90 top right, 90 bottom right, 119 bottom left, 148 bottom, 151 bottom right. Nicolas Régnault: p. 36-37, 45 left, 52 left. Jean Sonnet: p. 13 top, 66 top, 134, 136 left. Lila Vigy: p. 64-65.

Photography

Loïc Bezon: p. 57. Jacques Caillaut: p. 45 right, 67 bottom, 126 top, 157 bottom. Eric d'Hérouville: p. 18, 75, 87 left, 101, 102, 103 top, 113 left, 148 top. Jérôme Darblay: p. 92-93, 143, 157 top. Olivier de Lérins: p. 8, 24 top, 28, 40, 41, 48, 61, 66 bottom right, 70 left, 76 bottom left, 84, 106-107, 110, 124, 131 top, 140 centre, 151 top, 151 bottom left, 164-165. Henri del Olmo: p. 6 left, 23 top, 23 bottom left, 25, 29 left, 32, 36-37, 42, 45 left, 49, 51 top, 62 left, 63, 73 right, 88, 89 bottom right, 99, 104 bottom left, 109, 126 bottom, 136 right, 137, 144, 146, 161, 162, 163 bottom. Claire de Virieu: p. 39 bottom. Christophe Dugied: p. 6 right, 73 left. Yves Duronsoy: p. 12, 17, 20, 34 bottom left, 39 top, 43, 52 bottom left, 52 bottom right, 53 top, 60, 90 left, 121, 125, 135, 156, 166. Patrice Gavand: p. 13 top, 66 top, 134, 136 left. Joël Laiter: p. 38, 51 bottom right, 98, 128. Nadia Mackenzie: p. 24 bottom left. Nicolas Millet: p. 89 bottom left. Jean-Marc Palisse: p. 6 centre, 14-15. Giacomo Pietra: p. 72. Antoine Rozès: p. 64-65, 105, 112, 132-133. Christian Sarramon: p. 153 right. Ingalill Snitt: p. 100. Christine Ternynck: p. 46, 47. Bernard Touillon: p. 7, 11, 13 bottom, 16, 19 top and bottom, 21, 23 bottom right, 24 bottom right, 26-27, 29 right, 30, 31, 33, 34 top and bottom right, 35, 44, 51 bottom left, 52 top, 53 bottom, 54-55, 56, 58, 59, 62 right, 66 bottom left, 67 top, 68-69, 70 right, 71, 74, 76 top, 76 bottom right, 77, 78, 80-81, 82, 83, 85, 86, 87 right, 89 top, 90 right top and bottom, 94, 95, 96-97, 103 bottom, 104 top, 104 bottom right, 108, 111, 113 right, 114, 115, 116, 117, 119, 120, 122-123, 127, 129, 130, 131 bottom, 138-139, 140 left, 141, 142, 145, 147, 148 bottom, 149, 152, 154-155, 158, 159, 160, 163 top. Frédéric Vasseur: p. 4, 91, 151 bottom right, 153 left. Photothèque Hachette: p. 121 top.

Editor
Odile Perrard
Art editor
Sabine Houplain
Design
Séverine Morizet
Layout
Lawrence Bitterly
Research
Jean-Baptiste Roques
Remi Venture
Editorial assistance
Cécile Edrei

© Hachette Livre/Maisons Côté Sud 2002
This edition published by
Hachette Illustrated UK, Octopus Publishing Group,
2–4 Heron Quays, London E14 4JP

English translation produced by JMS Books LLP
Translation © Octopus Publishing Group

A CIP catalogue for this book is available from the British Library

ISBN: 1 84430 007 2

Printed by Tien Wah, Singapore